Stretching For Golfers

The complete 15-minute stretching and warm up routine that will help you improve your golf swing, score, and game

By David Nordmark

http://www.animal-kingdom-workouts.com

Golf Sketches Drawn By Jonathan Fesmire

https://www.elance.com/s/jfesmire/

http://jonfesmire.com/

Copyright 2012 by David Nordmark

Discover other Animal Kingdom Workout
Titles on Amazon
Lose Weight WITHOUT Dieting
Power Isotonics – The Complete Book of
Dynamic Self-Resistance Exercises
Power Isometrics
Natural Fitness - Natural Bodyweight Exercises
For Men and Women
Animal Workouts
The Ultimate Guide To Pushups

Disclaimer

The exercises and advice contained within this course may be too strenuous or dangerous for some people, and the reader(s) should consult a physician before engaging in them. The author and publisher of this course are not responsible in any manner whatsoever for any injury which may occur through reading and following the instructions herein.

Thank-you for downloading my book. Please REVIEW my book on Amazon. I appreciate your feedback so that I can make the next version even better. Thank-you so much!

Table Of Contents

Why Stretching Is Vital To Improving Your Golf Game

If you were to ask the average person to list the sports that they felt were the most taxing, it is doubtful that the sport of golf would be very high on anyone's list. To the uninitiated the sport of golf is a relaxing affair composed primarily of walking, putting, and the 19th hole. Unfortunately, too many golfers believe the same thing. They don't bother to stretch, thinking, "Hey, it's just golf". They simply don't bother to prepare their bodies to play the game the way tennis players or runners do. This is unfortunate as there is more to swinging a golf club than initially meets the eye, and this neglect can lead to injuries and pain in the long term. This is why performing some simple stretches before a game is a good idea.

A golf swing is made up of four components: the back swing, forward swing, ball strike and follow through. During the back swing the muscles are stretched like an elastic band, storing energy for the swing to come. The forward swing releases this energy with explosive force and it is this motion that determines how far the ball will travel. After the ball is hit all of those same muscles are stretched again until the follow through is completed.

All told, 22 separate muscles are involved in a golf swing. These include the following muscle groups:

- Core Muscles – used to twist the body and generate torque
- Hamstring Muscles – aid in proper posture and in stabilizing the back
- Quadriceps – needed to flex the knees
- Upper Back Muscles – assist in the rotation of the back swing and aid in maintaining an erect spine
- Shoulder Muscles – used to position the upper body and generate speed; the rotator cuffs are particularly vulnerable to injury
- Muscles in the Forearm, Wrists and Fingers – used to control the golf club

As you can see, there are a surprising number of muscles used when you swing a golf club. The next time someone tells you that they don't bother to stretch because "it's just golf", keep the above in mind.

Injuries that occur from playing golf can be placed in two categories. One category involves cumulative injuries, or injuries that result from overuse over time. Injuries such as rotator cuff tendonitis and golfer's elbow are examples of this. The second category involves more sudden, traumatic injuries. These are injuries that typically occur when you swing the club and BAM, there goes your back. These injuries are usually the result of muscle strains and nerve trauma. The chances of either occurring can be greatly reduced if proper stretches are performed before the activity.

Preparing your body in order to play the game of golf is the goal of this book. What follows within its pages is a simple stretching routine that will help mitigate the likelihood of either category occurring. It is made up of both dynamic and static stretches. Dynamic stretches being stretches that are based on movement. They are designed to loosen up your body while building up flexibility and strength. Static stretches are the more conventional type. They involve holding a position for a fix time in order to lengthen the muscle. Both types are valuable in order to prepare your body.

The first exercise in the routine, however, is not a stretch at all. Known as Meridian Breathing, it is a deep breathing exercise. It is the kind of exercise that you are more likely to find in a martial arts class than a golfing book (unless it's this one, of course). The reason this stretching routine starts with this is that it has been proven that breathing deeply through the nose and completely filling your lungs has a calming effect on the body. This energizes and relaxes you, which is the state you want to be in when you go onto to the rest of the routine, not to mention playing your round of golf.

Here's a tip when performing this breathing exercise. As you do it, consciously think of your muscles and tell them to relax. Imagine that your muscles are frozen, but as you perform the movement they begin to melt.

Always remember that your mind controls your muscles. Take advantage of this.

The next two exercises are examples of dynamic stretches. The Tai Chi Waist Turner is great for warming up your body, in particular your spine. From then on there are a mixture of dynamic and static stretches all designed to prepare your body for the game of golf.

When performing this routine it is important to have the proper mental attitude. Most people hate stretching. They see it as a chore, something to be gotten over with as quickly as possible. You can see it in their faces, which are typically contorted in expressions of pain and discomfort as they force themselves to perform stretches they don't want to do in the first place. This is precisely the wrong way to approach stretching. A tight and angry mind leads to tight and angry muscles. It is impossible to stretch properly if you are in such a mental state. When you force a stretch to the point of pain, injury is typically the result. Do not do this, ever!

Instead, always breathe deeply through your nose and only stretch until you feel a slight resistance from your muscles. When you reach this point hold the stretch with a smiling, happy face (that's a yoga expression, btw) until you feel your muscles relax. This is how stretching should be, a pleasant, relaxing experience that helps you fine-tune your body. It should be something you enjoy doing, not an activity to be avoided.

The stretching routine contained within these pages should be all you need to prepare your body so that you can play a great game of golf. However, if some parts of your body are extra stiff, I've included some supplementary stretches that can help with these problem areas. Feel free to add these stretches to the main routine as you see fit.

If you have any specific questions, comments, or suggestions you can reach me through the contact form on my website at www.animal-kingdom-workouts.com. This book is largely a result of comments I received from golfers who read my earlier, larger book *Animal Stretching*. I'm always looking to improve my books and any comments you have would be most welcome (in fact, this book has already been improved based on reader suggestions). Also, if you like this book and found it useful I always appreciate getting reviews on Amazon. Even a few sentences would help me out a lot. Thanks in advance and I hope you find this stretching routine for golfers helpful!

The 15-Minute Stretching Routine

Meridian Breathing

In order to play your best game of golf you need to be relaxed. There is no better way to relax your body than by performing deep breathing exercises. All forms of ancient exercise, from places as diverse as China and India, put tremendous emphasis on the importance of breathing. Breathing deeply through your nose has a calming yet energizing effect on the body. Meridian Breathing is not only a great way to prepare for your golf game but it can also be done anytime throughout the day when you feel the need to focus yourself.

1. Stand with your feet shoulder width apart and your hands by your sides, palms out.
2. Slowly breathe in through your nose as you raise your hands above your head. Keep your arms straight with your palms out.
3. When your arms cross at the top start to exhale through your nose as you lower your arms to the starting position.
4. Repeat this circular motion with your arms 10 times.

Additional Notes

- Always remember to keep your palms turned out (So they are facing the ceiling) when you raise your hands.

- To the Chinese this exercise reconnects your meridians and helps to get your internal energy focused.
- With this breathing exercise along with the next three it is very important to use your imagination and mind. As you breathe in imagine that you are breathing in white, vibrant energy. Imagine that it is filling you and revitalizing you. As you exhale imagine that you are breathing out dark, negative energy.

Tai Chi Waist Turner

This exercise not only increases the flexibility in your waist and spine, but it also massages your internal organs as well.

1. Stand straight up with your knees slightly bent and your feet shoulder width apart. Your arms should be hanging loosely by your sides.
2. Turn your head and body to one side, then twist your body to the opposite. Move fast enough so that you generate the centrifugal force necessary to swing your arms. At the end of each twist your hands should gently slap your lower back and kidneys.
3. Do 50 to 100 reps.

Additional Notes

- This movement will loosen up your waist while massaging your internal organs and re-aligning your spine. This is vital if you wish to swing a golf club properly.
- You should never consciously move your arms. The only thing moving them is the force generated by the twisting motion.
- The slapping of your arms and hands against your body is what generates the massage and is very beneficial for your internal organs.

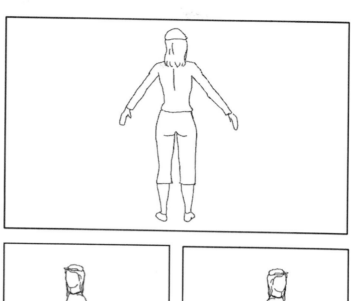

Grounded Back Twist

1. Take a wide stance, double shoulder length at minimum.
2. Bend your knees while keeping your back straight and place the palms of your hands on the inside of your knees. Use your hands to gently push your knees backwards.
3. Turn your head so that you are looking over your right shoulder. Twist your upper body at the same time as if you are trying to look at the wall behind you.
4. Hold for 5 seconds then repeat on the opposite side.
5. Repeat this 5 times.

Additional Notes

- This will stretch your lower back and will also help ground your energy. You will feel a greater sense of calm and focus when you have finished this exercise.
- Breathe in through your nose as you look over you shoulder. Exhale when you look forward.
- Primary areas worked - lower back

Straight Arm Stretch

1. Interlace your fingers in front of you and extend your arms with the palms out.
2. Hold this stretch for 15 seconds.
3. Relax, then raise your hands above your head. Extend your arms again and hold for another 15 seconds.

Additional Notes

- You should feel a stretch in your shoulders, upper back, hands, fingers, forearms and wrists.

Standing Waist Stretch With Golf Club

1. Stand straight up with your feet shoulder width apart and your toes pointed forward.
2. Take a golf club and hold it over your head with both hands.
3. Keeping your pelvis steady, bend as far as you can to the right.
4. Stop when you feel a gentle stretch on your left side. Hold this position for 10 to 15 seconds.
5. Slowly rise to the starting position and repeat on the opposite side.
6. Place one hand on your hip as you raise the opposite arm above your head.

Additional Notes

- This stretch will also build strength along the side of your body as well.
- Keep you knees slightly bent at all times.

Shoulder Rotation Stretch

1. With your feet shoulder-width apart hold your left elbow with your right hand. Keeping your knees slightly bent you will want to stand as if you're addressing the golf ball.
2. Keeping your left thumb pointed up, bend your left wrist towards your left thumb.
3. Rotate your trunk to the right as if you're about to tee off.
4. Use your right hand to apply pressure on your left elbow until you feel a gentle stretch in your back.
5. Hold this stretch for 15 seconds.
6. To stretch your trailing (right) shoulder, grab your right elbow with your left hand.
7. Now rotate your trunk to the left as if you have just completed a follow through after hitting a golf ball. Hold this stretch for 15 seconds.

Trunk Rotation With Golf Club

1. Hook your arms with the golf club at the elbows. The club should now be lengthwise across your back.
2. Rotate your trunk and head to the left and hold a gentle stretch for 15 seconds.
3. Repeat in the opposite direction.

Additional Notes

- Do not swing or bounce into this stretch as this could result in injury. It should be performed in one fluid motion.
- This stretch can also be performed while sitting down. However, this will likely reduce the effectiveness of the stretch in your lower back.
- This is a great stretch to do while actually playing a round of golf as it can be done easily while you wait for other players.

Hip Stretch With Club

1. While holding onto your golf club with your right hand for support, kneel on your right knee.
2. Gently lean forward. By doing so you should feel your weight shifting onto your left leg.
3. Keep your back straight and abdominal muscles tight at all times.
4. You should feel a stretch in the front of your right hip and thigh.
5. Hold this stretch for 15 seconds.
6. Repeat this stretch for your left side.

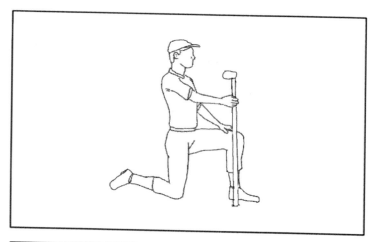

Standing Calf Stretch

1. Lean against a wall with your forearms, your head resting on your hands.
2. Bring one leg forward close to the wall while stretching the other leg out straight behind you.
3. Keeping the heel of the stretched leg on the ground, slowly move your hips forward while keeping your back straight.

Additional Notes

- You can stretch your Achilles tendon as well using this stretch by lowering your hips and bending your stretched knee slightly.
- Keep your heel on the ground at all times.
- Remember that you only want to feel a slight stretch in the Achilles tendon.

Standing Hamstring Stretch

1. Begin standing with your feet shoulder width apart and pointed forward.
2. With your knees slightly bent begin to slowly bend forward from the hips.
3. Bend as far forward as you can until you feel a gentle stretch in the back of your knees.

Additional Notes

- You should feel this stretch mainly in your hamstrings and behind the knees.
- Your back may get a slight stretch as well.

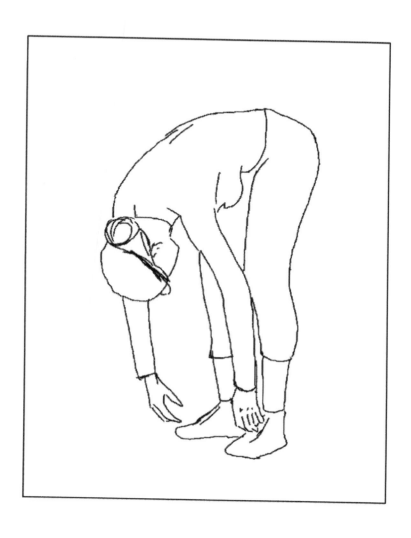

Sitting Groin Stretch

1. Sit on the floor with the soles of your feet together while grabbing them with your hands. Your heels should be a comfortable distance (for you) from your crotch.
2. Gently pull yourself forward until you feel an easy stretch in your groin area. Concentrate on keeping your back straight while looking straight ahead of you. The initial movement should be coming from your hips, not by rounding your head and shoulders.
3. Perform an easy stretch for 25 seconds.

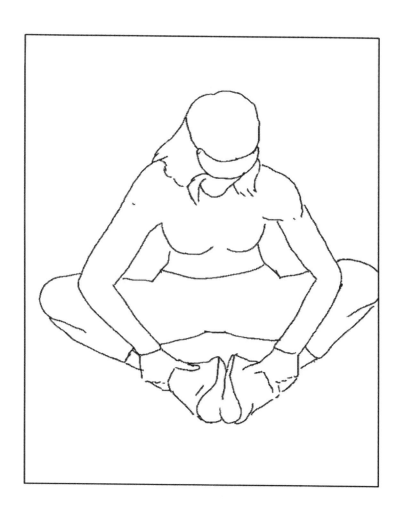

Hamstring Stretch With Club

1. Stand in front of a step, low table or bench.
2. Place your golf club behind your shoulders. Hold onto it with both hands.
3. Place your right foot on the bench with your knee slightly bent.
4. Keeping your spine straight bend forward at the hips until you feel a gentle stretch in the back of your right thigh.
5. While holding this stretch for 15 seconds, gently rotate your back and shoulders once to the right and once to the left.
6. Repeat this stretch on the opposite side.

Forearm and Wrist Stretch

1. Get down on your hands and knees.
   Keep your arms straight with your
   thumbs on the outside and your fingers
   pointed towards your knees.
2. Start to lean backwards until you feel an
   easy stretch. Hold for 20 seconds.

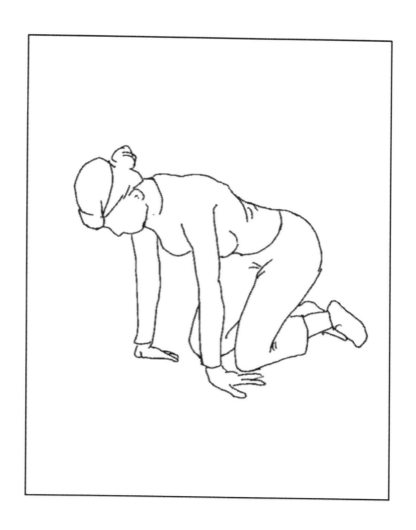

Supplemental Stretches

What follows are some additional stretches that you may find useful. The basic stretching routine should be enough for most golfers. However, if you are experiencing extra stiffness adding a few of these exercises to the basic routine is sure to be beneficial.

Additional Stretches for the Arms

Clasped Hand Turns

1. Bring your right hand in front of you with your palm facing outward to the right.
2. Bring your left palm, facing to the left, over your right hand and clasp your hands together.
3. Bring your clenched hands in towards your chest by rotating from your elbows then extend them outwards again.
4. Repeat this motion 5 to 10 times.

Additional Notes

- You may find it difficult to keep you hands clasped tightly together as your perform this motion. If this is the case feel free to loosen your grasp. Just try and keep your hands clenched together as best you can.
- This joint loosening exercise is also extremely effective in combating Carpel Tunnel Syndrome.

"Praying" Stretch

1. Kneel down on the floor with your knees separated.
2. Reach forward as far as you can with both arms and grab the mat or carpet if you can.
3. Pull backwards with straight arms and back while keeping your palms pressed down.
4. Hold for 15 seconds.

Additional Notes

- You should feel this stretch in your arms, shoulders and upper back. You can also do this stretch with one arm at a time if one arm is slightly tighter than the other.

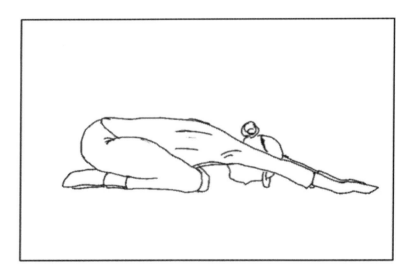

Additional Stretches for the Shoulders

Gymnastic Shoulder Shrugs

1. Begin standing with your feet shoulder width apart.
2. Raise your hands above your head with your palms pointed down.
3. Shrug your shoulders up, hold for a second or two, then relax.
4. Do 10 to 15 reps.

Additional Notes

- When you bring your hands above your head imagine that you are holding onto a large beach ball.

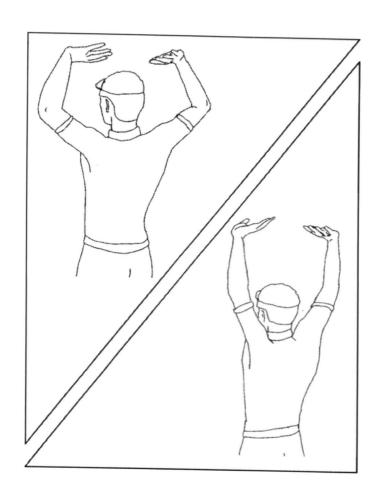

Gymnastic Shoulder Pulls

1. Begin with your feet shoulder width apart and your knees slightly bent.
2. Imagine that you are grabbing onto 2 buckets of water that you then lift up to your armpits.
3. From this position shrug your shoulders up so that they almost squeeze your head. Hold for a couple of seconds and release.
4. Repeat 10 times.

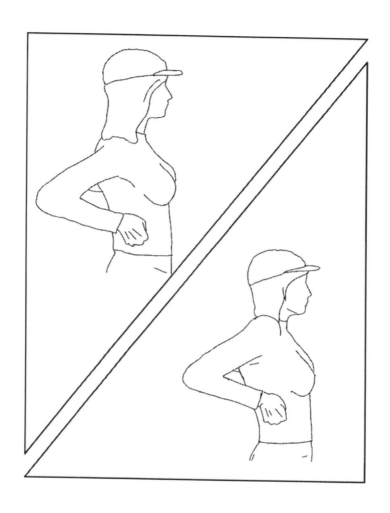

Back Shoulder Stretch

1. With your left elbow in the air, reach behind your back with your left hand.
2. With your right elbow towards the floor, reach up with your right hand, palm out, and grab your left hand with your fingers.
3. Hold this stretch for 15 seconds.

Additional Notes

- If you are not flexible enough for your hands to meet behind your back make up the distance by using a towel or a golf club (although a towel is preferable). As you gain in flexibility inch up the towel, bringing your hands closer together, until you no longer need it.

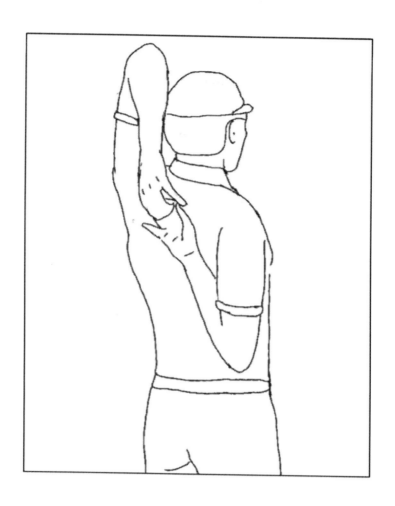

Additional Stretches for the Back

Secretary Stretch

This movement will provide a nice stretch for your lower back, side, and the top of the hip. Your upper back, head, shoulders, and elbows should remain flat on the floor at all times.

1. Lie flat on your back with your knees bent and together and your feet flat on the floor. Interlace your fingers and place them behind your head.
2. Bring your left knee over your right leg.
3. Use your left leg to gently pull your right leg towards the floor. You should feel a good stretch along the side of you hip and in your lower back. Hold the stretch for 30 seconds while breathing calmly and slowly.

Additional Notes

1. Do not try and force your right leg down so that it touches the floor. Only bring it down as far as you need to in order to feel a relaxing stretch.
2. Repeat with the other side, crossing your right leg over your left and bringing it down to the floor.

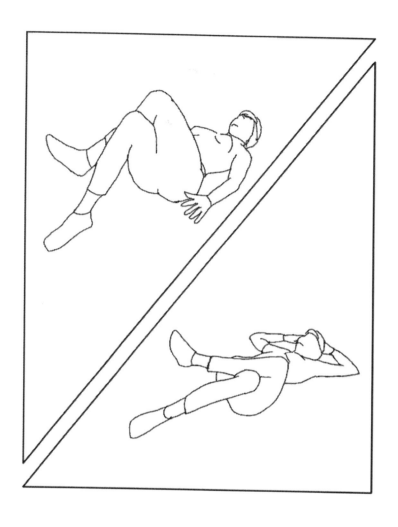

Cobra Stretch

1. Begin lying on the ground with your heals together. Your eyes should be looking forward, not at the ground.
2. Place your palms on the ground underneath your shoulders.
3. Straighten your arms and look up. This will raise your stomach off the ground. Keep your hips on the ground.

Additional Notes

- This exercise will stretch your stomach and relieve tension from your back. Take it easy when first performing this stretch as most people are not used to back bending.

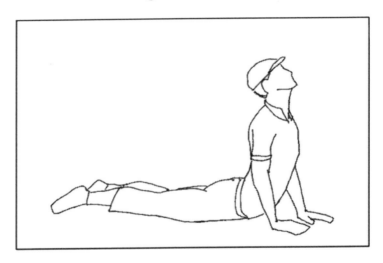

Spinal Twist

1. Sit on the floor with your right leg out straight.
2. Bend your left leg and cross it over your right leg. Place the left foot on the outside of your right knee.
3. Bend your right elbow and rest it on the outside of your upper left thigh. Keep your left arm on the floor for support.
4. Slowly turn your head to look over your left shoulder while rotating your upper body.

Additional Notes

- You should feel this stretch in your lower back and hip.
- Do not hold your breath while performing this stretch. Breathe easily and naturally.

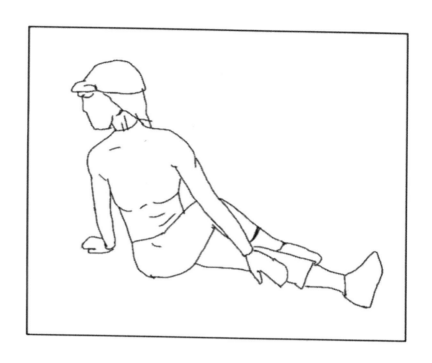

Additional Stretches for the Legs and Hips

Upper Hamstring And Hip Stretch

1. Sit on the floor with your feet extended in front of you.
2. Bend your right knee at 90 degrees and place it on top of your still extended left leg.
3. Bend forward and grab your right ankle with your left hand while wrapping your right arm around your right knee and leg.
4. Gently pull your right leg towards your chest. Make sure that you pull your leg as one unit in order to protect your knee.
5. You should feel this stretch in your upper hamstrings and hip. Hold this stretch for 20 seconds then repeat on the opposite side.

Additional Notes

•   If you wish you can lean your back against a wall for support.

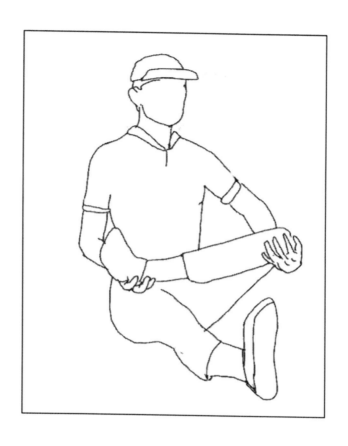

Forward Rows

1. Begin with your feet shoulder width apart.
2. Cross your forearms so that your palms are facing upwards and your wrists are parallel to each other.
3. Bend forward at the waist so that your arms are just below your waist. This is the starting position.
4. Exhale through your nose as you bend further at the waist bringing your arms towards the floor.
5. Inhale as you bend upwards at the waist again and you move back to the starting position.
6. Do this movement slowly. The result is a gentle rowing motion.
7. Repeat 10 times.

Additional Notes

- This is a great stretch for your hamstrings and lower back.
- If you have tight hamstrings bend your knees. This will relieve tension from the lower back.
- Never raise your back beyond parallel to the floor when performing this movement.
- From the side your elbows should almost be making a circular motion. They come away from your legs as your bend forward, then come towards your legs during the upward motion.

Standing Leg-Under Abductor Stretch

1. Lean forward and grab onto a chair or similar object for balance.
2. Cross one foot behind the other and slide that foot away from your body, keeping your legs straight.
3. Slowly bend your front leg to lower your body.

Additional Notes

- You can regulate the intensity of the stretch by using the bent leg to lower the body.
- You should feel this in your hips, ankles, and the side of your leg.

Golf Form - Tips To Avoid Injury

Many golf injuries are the result of poor form over time. Keep the following tips in mind for the next time you play.

To avoid back injury:

- During the backswing try to rotate your shoulder and hip by about the same degree.
- Try to keep the spine vertical during the follow-through as this lessens the chances of hyperextending it.

To avoid shoulder and elbow injury:

- Try shortening the length of your backswing by ending with the club head at a 1 o'clock rather than a 3 o'clock position.
- Study the mechanics of proper swing with a pro.
- Slow the velocity of the swing in order to produce less shock to the arm when the ball is struck.

To avoid hand, wrist and elbow injuries:

- Use larger and softer club grips
- Use a neutral grip to hold the club
- Select irons with larger heads and lower vibration
- Graphite shafts can lessen vibration
- Select the correct club length

About the Author

David Nordmark has a life long interest in health and fitness. In the past he has participated in such sports as soccer, basketball and hockey. He also was once an avid runner and weightlifter, but has since come to his senses. Today he mainly does natural exercises like Yoga and the Body Weight exercises found on his website, www.animal-kingdom-workouts.com.

He currently lives in beautiful Vancouver, British Columbia Canada, although he really wouldn't mind living somewhere else during the winter. He's currently working on making that dream a reality.

If you have any questions for him, feel free to contact him using the contact form which can be found on this website. Here's the link: http://www.animal-kingdom-workouts.com/contactme.html

One Last Thing

When you turn the page, Kindle will give you
the opportunity to rate the book and share
your thoughts through an automatic feed to
your Facebook and Twitter accounts. If you
believe your friends would get something
valuable out of this book, I'd be honored if
you'd post your thoughts. As well, if you liked
the book, I'd be eternally grateful if you posted
a review on Amazon. Thank-you once again
and I hope you enjoyed the book!

Made in the USA
San Bernardino, CA
10 March 2017